# ODDS AND EVENS

# A NUMBERS BOOK

# ODDS and EVENS

## by Heidi Goennel

**TAMBOURINE BOOKS**
**NEW YORK**

Library of Congress Cataloging in Publication Data

Goennel, Heidi. Odds and evens: A numbers book/Heidi Goennel. p. cm.
Summary:  Counts to thirteen in terms such as one-horse
town, six of one, eight ball, and baker's dozen.
1. Counting—Juvenile literature. [1. Counting.] I. Title.
QA113.G64 1994 513.2'11— dc20 [E] 93-15420 CIP AC
ISBN 0 - 688 -12918 - 8. — ISBN 0 - 688 -12919 - 6 (lib.)
1 3 5 7 9 10 8 6 4 2
First edition

To Peter

1 • 2 • 3 • 4 • 5 • 6 • 7

# A one-horse town

8 • 9 • 10 • 11 • 12 • 13

1 • 2 • 3 • 4 • 5 • 6 • 7

# Two in the bush

8 • 9 • 10 • 11 • 12 • 13

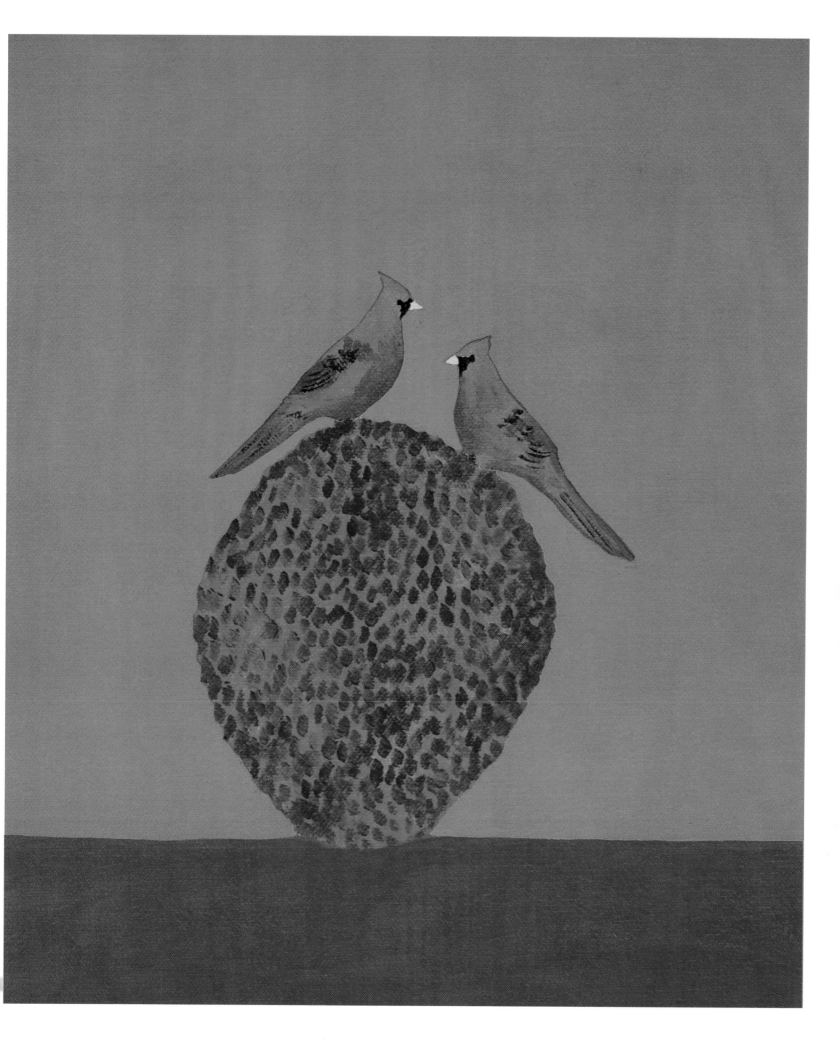

1 • 2 • 3 • 4 • 5 • 6 • 7

# Three blind mice

8 • 9 • 10 • 11 • 12 • 13

1 · 2 · 3 · 4 · 5 · 6 · 7

# A four-leaf clover

8 · 9 · 10 · 11 · 12 · 13

1 • 2 • 3 • 4 • 5 • 6 • 7

# The five senses

8 • 9 • 10 • 11 • 12 • 13

1 · 2 · 3 · 4 · 5 · 6 · 7

# Six of one and half-a-dozen of the other

8 · 9 · 10 · 11 · 12 · 13

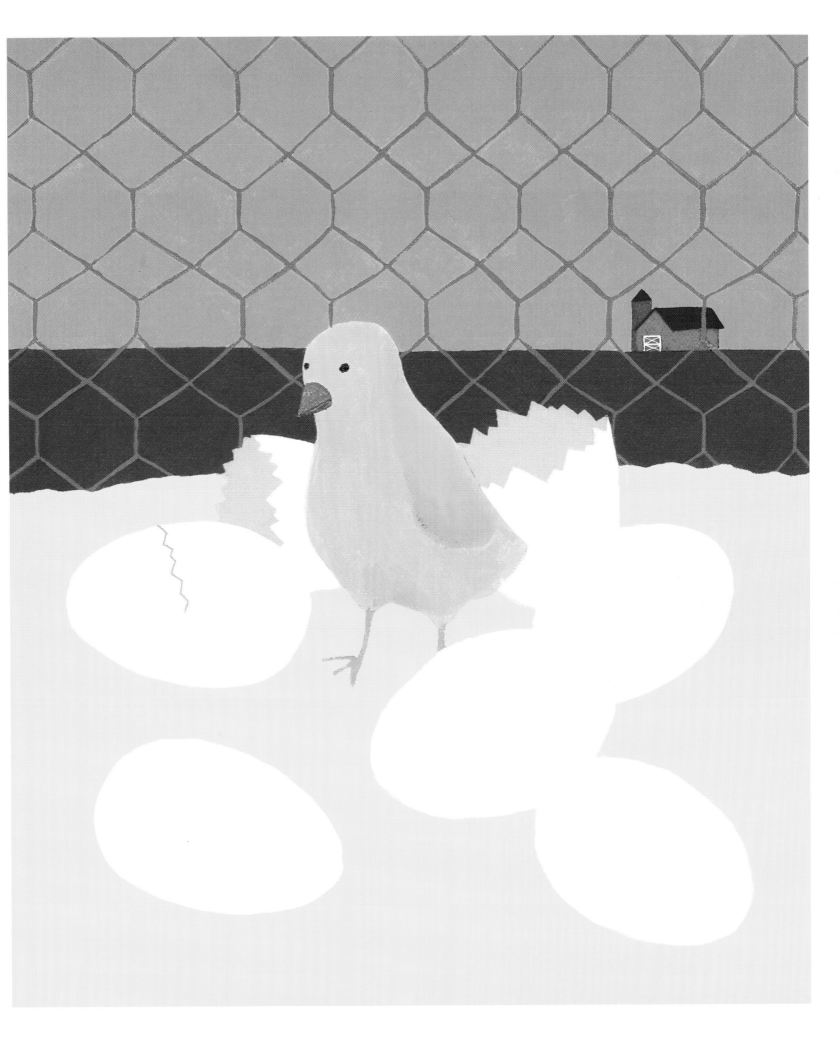

1 • 2 • 3 • 4 • 5 • 6 • 7

# Seventh heaven

8 • 9 • 10 • 11 • 12 • 13

1 · 2 · 3 · 4 · 5 · 6 · 7

# Behind the eight ball

8 · 9 · 10 · 11 · 12 · 13

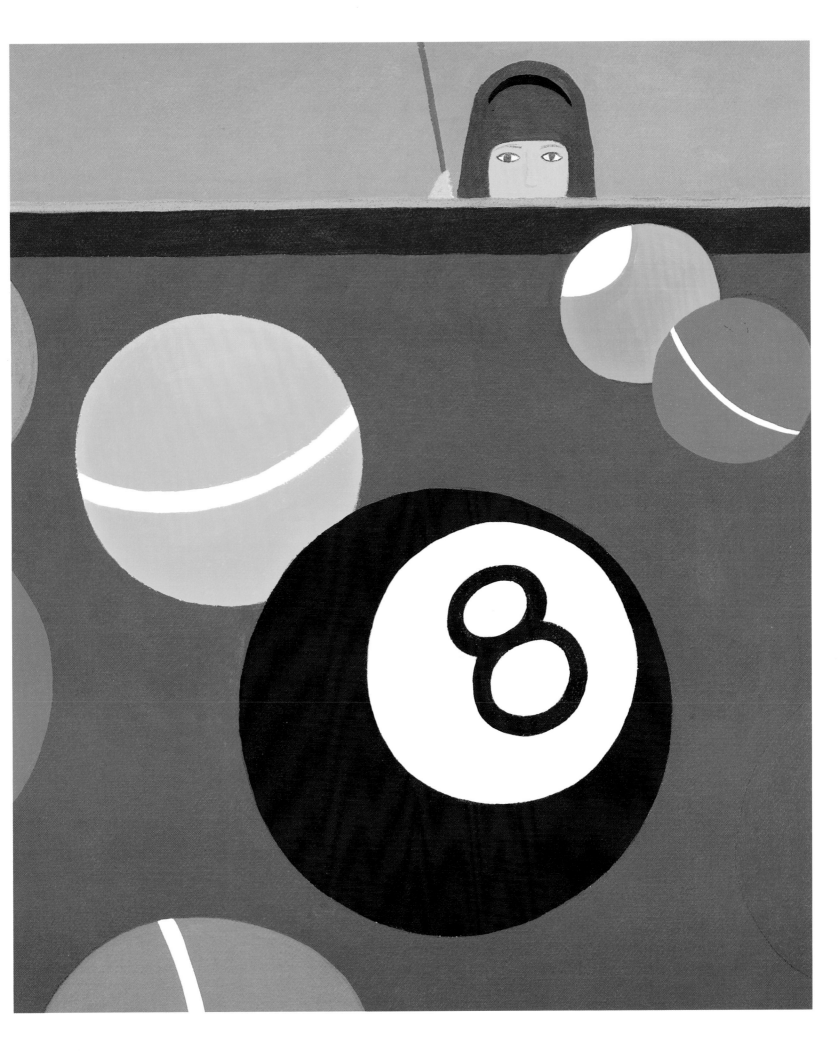

1 • 2 • 3 • 4 • 5 • 6 • 7

# A cat has nine lives

8 • 9 • 10 • 11 • 12 • 13

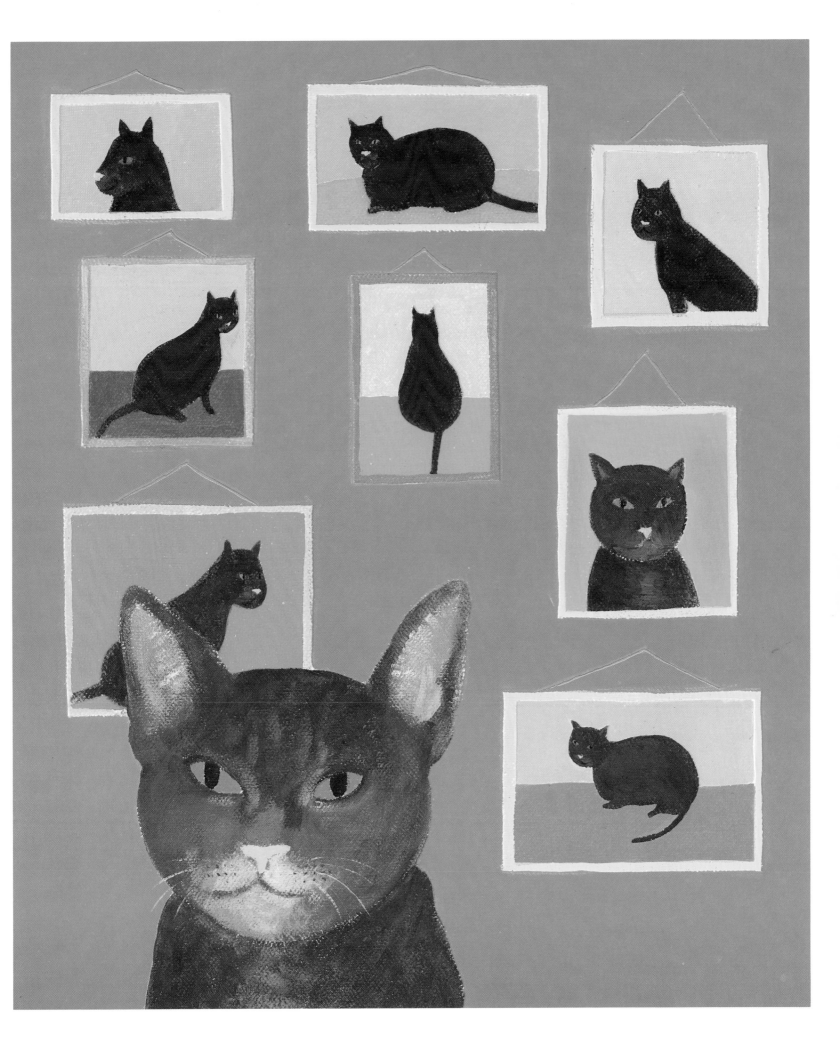

1 • 2 • 3 • 4 • 5 • 6 • 7

# Ten-gallon hat

8 • 9 • 10 • 11 • 12 • 13

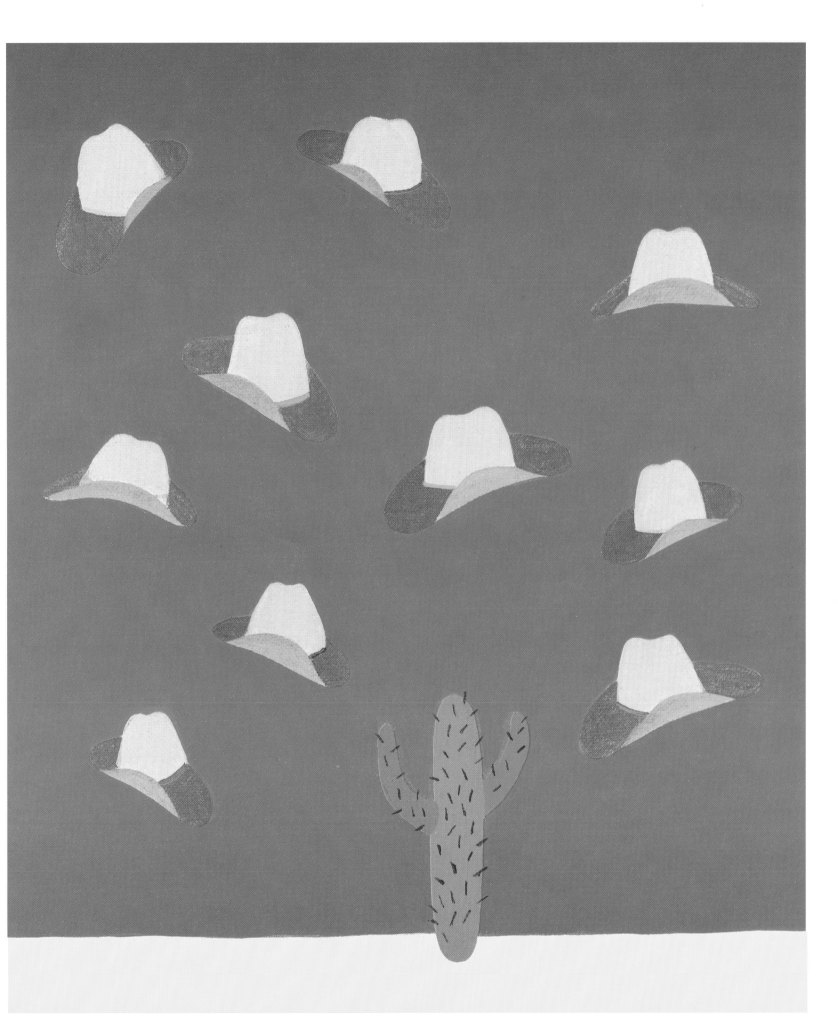

1 • 2 • 3 • 4 • 5 • 6 • 7

# The eleventh hour

8 • 9 • 10 • 11 • 12 • 13

1 · 2 · 3 · 4 · 5 · 6 · 7

# The clock strikes twelve

8 · 9 · 10 · 11 · 12 · 13

1 • 2 • 3 • 4 • 5 • 6 • 7

# A baker's dozen

8 • 9 • 10 • 11 • 12 • 13

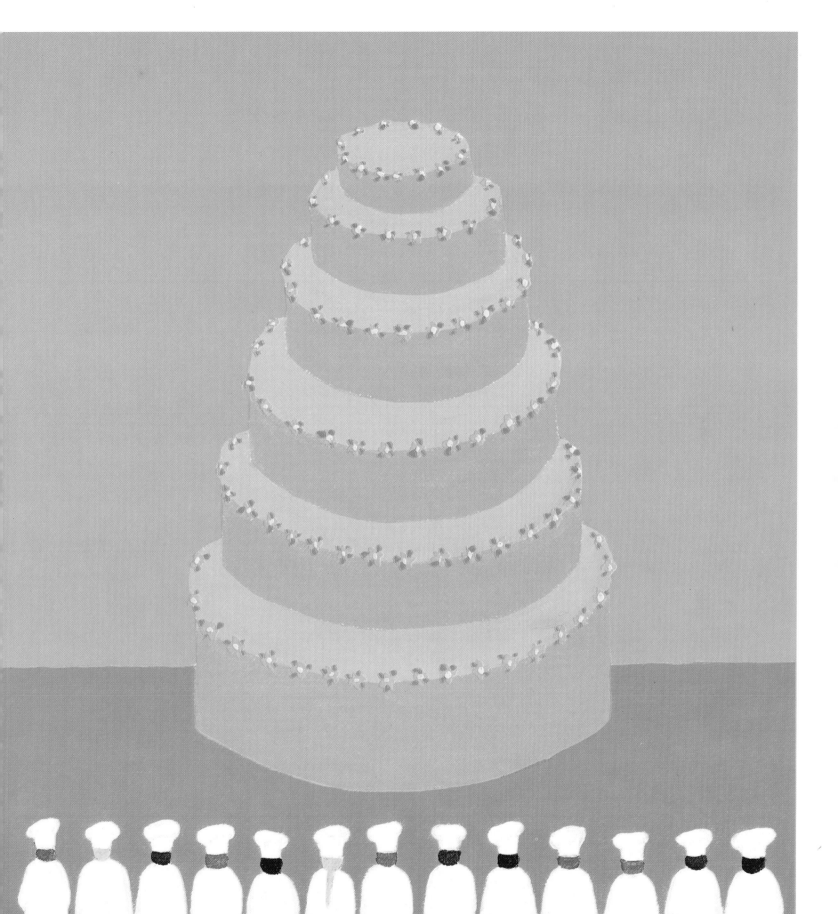

1 · 2 · 3 · 4 · 5 · 6 · 7

8 · 9 · 10 · 11 · 12 · 13